SUGGESTIONS FOR GROUP LEADERS

1. THE ROOM Discourage people from sitting [...] need to be equally involved.

2. HOSPITALITY Tea or coffee on arrival can [...] the end too, to encourage people to talk inf[...] ambitious, taking it in turns to bring a desse[...] hospitality is OK!) with coffee at the end.

3. THE START If group members don't know each other well, some kind of 'icebreaker' might be helpful. For example, you might invite people to share something quite secular (where they grew up, holidays, hobbies, significant object, etc.) or something more 'spiritual' (one thing I like and one thing I dislike about my church/denomination). Place a time limit on this exercise.

4. PREPARING THE GROUP Take the group into your confidence, e.g. 'I've never done this before', or 'I've led lots of groups and each one has contained surprises'. Sharing vulnerability is designed to encourage all members to see the success of the group as their responsibility. Encourage those who know that they talk easily to ration their contributions. You might introduce a fun element by producing a bell which all must obey instantly. Encourage the reticent to speak at least once or twice – however briefly. Explain that there are no 'right' answers and that among friends it is fine to say things that you are not sure about – to express half-formed ideas. If individuals choose to say nothing, that is all right too.

5. THE MATERIAL Encourage members to read next week's chapter before the meeting. It helps enormously if each group member has their own personal copy of this booklet – hence the reduced rate when 5 or more copies are ordered. There is no need to consider all the questions. A lively exchange of views is what matters, so be selective. You can always spread a session over two or more meetings, if the discussion is very lively! You might decide to replay all or part of the CD/audiotape – the closing reflection for example – at the end.

For some questions you might start with a few minutes' silence to make jottings. Or you might ask members to talk in sub-groups of two or three, before sharing with the whole group.

6. PREPARATION Decide beforehand whether to distribute (or ask people to bring) paper, pencils, hymn books, etc. If possible, ask people in advance to read a Bible passage or lead in prayer, so that they can prepare.

7. TIMING Try to start on time and make sure you stick fairly closely to your stated finishing time.

8. USING THE CD/AUDIOTAPE Some groups will play the 14 minute piece at the beginning of the meeting. Other groups will prefer to play it at the end – or to play 7/8 minutes at the beginning and the rest halfway through the meeting. The track markers (on the CD only) will help you find any section very easily, including the Closing Reflections. Or you can ignore these markers altogether, if you prefer.

A word-by-word TRANSCRIPT booklet of the CD/audiotape is available. GROUP LEADERS may find this helpful as they prepare. In addition, reading the transcript can help some group members feel more confident about joining in the discussion, while others may wish to go over the recorded material at leisure after the session. (*See centre pages of this booklet.*)

SESSION 1

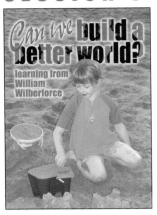

SLAVERY:
then and now

In 1807, after lengthy and fierce debate, the British Parliament passed an Act abolishing the slave trade. Two hundred years later we celebrate the life, vision and work of the Christian politician who drove this measure through in the face of strong opposition. It is appropriate that *York Courses* should produce a course built around his achievements, for William Wilberforce was a great Yorkshireman. He attended school in Pocklington, near York. In 1780 he was elected MP for Hull (now in the York Diocese) and in 1784 he became MP for Yorkshire itself.

This course uses the vision and achievements of Wilberforce as a springboard, but it is not a history lesson. Our concern will be to consider the implications of the faith which motivated him *then*, for our lives as disciples of Jesus Christ *today*.

As we seek to build a better world, what can we learn from the principles which guided him and the vision which inspired him? This is the vital question we shall pursue.

The slave trade then

In eighteenth century Britain cheap labour – slave labour – was an accepted and important part of the economic landscape. A great deal depended on it and it was justified on various grounds.

- *The economy depends on it.* Many people assumed that the British economy simply could not flourish without the slave trade. We needed slaves – so what was the point of debate?

- *Greed.* If fortunes were there to be made at other people's expense, so much the worse for other people.

- *Inertia.* When attitudes and actions are both profitable and deeply embedded, the vision and energy required for radical change are immense.

- *They are different from us.* As a child I visited Kew Gardens where I saw an exhibition of 'native workers' on a plantation. I recall feeling worried about the long hours and terrible conditions, but a well-meaning adult told me that 'the natives don't feel things like we do.' The implication was that they were somehow less human than we are. I can't recall who said this, but I suspect he believed his own propaganda. I do recall that it quietened my fears just a bit – and left me wondering if it were true.

These attitudes and beliefs played an important role in persuading ordinary decent Britons that slavery was necessary and tolerable. They were buttressed by other 'bluff arguments which had a certain cogency – it saved

> In 1800 there were an estimated 800,000 negro slaves in Spanish America and about 300,000 in Jamaica... From West Africa the volume of trade was enormous and, as is well-known, the conditions under which the slaves were shipped across the Atlantic were appalling.
>
> *Peter Hinchliff*

African prisoners who would otherwise be massacred, or victims of famine who would die anyway' (Professor John McManners).

The slave trade now

When I first came across the modern anti-Slavery movement, I was surprised. Surely the slave trade ended in 1807 and slavery itself was outlawed in 1833, just after Wilberforce died? It's certainly true that William Wilberforce, and the growing band of people who thought like him, *did* win a famous victory. We are right to celebrate. But it remains true that there are millions of slaves in today's world.

Modern slavery embraces forced labour, bonded labour, slavery based on descent, forced marriage, and child labour. In West Africa, parents in Benin sometimes face the heartbreak of selling some of their children in order to feed and clothe the rest. These children will probably be taken to another country (e.g. Gabon) where they may be forced to work up to 18 hours each day.

The tragic problem of modern slavery is not confined to Africa. Many people in Britain today are:
- Forced to work by threats
- Owned or controlled
- Dehumanised – treated as a commodity
- Constrained – their freedom of movement is restricted

Various groups fulfil these tragic criteria:
- **Sex Slaves** This is the most publicised aspect of modern slavery in Britain. Young women, often from Eastern Europe, are tricked into becoming prostitutes or domestic drudges. Promises are made and good, well-paid jobs are held out as bait. On arrival, many of these women find themselves trapped in an unsavoury – and sometimes terrifying – world of pimps, exploitation, threats and exhaustion.
- **Illegal Labour** It is widely recognised, even by the Government, that many people do come to Britain – and stay in Britain – illegally.

In April 1999 the Labour administration introduced a minimum wage. This was opposed by the Conservative Party which argued that it would place too great a burden on companies, especially small businesses. In fact the system seems to have worked well, as the Conservatives now agree. But illegal workers have no such protection. They can be – and are – exploited as domestic drudges or casual workers.

The world was shocked when 21 cocklepickers drowned in Morecambe Bay on 5 February 2004. They were working at night – long hours for low pay – unprotected by health and safety regulations.

- **Unfair Trade** The Fairtrade movement was launched some years ago to combat unfair trading practices. The Christian organisation *Traidcraft* has been a key player since it was founded in 1979. The movement continues to grow rapidly. Aware that we in the West exploit workers in the developing world (often unwittingly), this movement's main concern is to ensure a fair day's pay for a fair day's work. It started as a fringe movement but its growing popularity ensures that large supermarkets now stock fairly traded goods, and some multi-national companies are developing fairtrade product ranges.

The variety of fairtrade goods is steadily increasing and includes clothes, jewellery and wine, as well as food, coffee and tea. All this is very encouraging. It proves that today – as in the lifetime of William Wilberforce – individuals, groups and churches can make a real difference. But many activists in the Fairtrade movement work on a wider canvas too. They know that what matters most is the establishment of rules and codes of trading practice on the world stage. So they lobby politicians.

Many politicians welcome such lobbying, for it strengthens their hand. It is certainly not a case of good fairtraders versus wicked politicians. Most politicians enter the political arena genuinely wanting to make a difference. They *want* to build a better world. But those involved in these matters – politicians and others – know that the issues are extremely complex. It is sometimes difficult to help one group without harming another. Negotiators and legislators need the wisdom of Solomon, the patience of Job – and the prayers of the Church.

They also need the inspiration and courage which can be drawn from those who have won fierce political battles in the past. Men like Lord Shaftesbury who picked up and ran with many of the concerns of William Wilberforce – famously forcing through legislation to protect child labourers. Women like Elizabeth Fry, who worked tirelessly to improve conditions for prisoners; Hannah More, a friend of Wilberforce and educational pioneer; and Eglantyne Jebb, founder of *Save the Children*.

Christians do not have a monopoly on social justice. Nonetheless, it remains true that these and many, many others were – and still are – motivated, inspired and strengthened by their Christian faith in seeking to build a much better world.

QUESTIONS FOR GROUPS

BIBLE READING: Micah 6:8

Reminder (see page 1). We include a wide range of questions to suit the needs of various groups. You will probably not have time to consider them all!

---

1. William Wilberforce is still an inspiration for many. Pick out from history, or from personal experience, two other people who have inspired you. How has this worked in your life?

2. The phrase 'compassion fatigue' is sometimes heard e.g. 'I gave money following the Asian tsunami. Then there was the earthquake in Pakistan. And now... I have my own money worries and can't be expected to solve the world's problems'.

   (a) Can you identify with this, or are you impatient with this attitude? **(b)** Do you worry that the money is wasted, or do you have confidence in our charities (non-governmental organisations/NGOs)? **(c)** Ask group members who have taken part in door-to-door or street collections for charity to share their experiences. **(d)** Why do some disasters tug at our heartstrings more readily than others? Are you more likely to give to 'people like us' as some commentators suggest?

3. Re-read my Kew Gardens experience (page 2). What do you make of the adult's comment?

4. *Re-read Micah 6:8.* Inertia and lack of vision by the British public 250 years ago kept slaves in chains. Can you look back and think of issues or incidents of which you now feel ashamed because you did nothing? Or circumstances which you worked hard to change?

5. Share your views on, and experience of, the Fairtrade movement. Are you willing to pay more for goods which carry the Fairtrade logo? If you believe in fairtrade, how can you (as an individual, group or church) encourage its growth?

6. Some commentators believe that, with an ageing population, Britain will depend on immigrants more and more e.g. to fix our plumbing and our health. What do you think about this? What effect might this have on the 'sending' countries?

7. *Read Exodus 23:9.* Describe an experience when you felt alone and afraid. Now imagine what it must be like to find yourself in a threatening situation in a strange country, with no friends or money (see Sex Slaves page 3).

8. Do you agree that the list on page 3 really does sum up 'slavery' in modern Britain? Have you experienced any or all of these situations at some point in your own lives? Or do you know people who have?

9. *Read Romans 13:5-7.*
   (a) 'Most politicians enter the political arena really wanting to make a difference' (page 4). Do you agree or do you believe that William Wilberforce was a shining exception? **(b)** What can we ordinary people do to improve the way we are governed? **(c)** Should the Church get involved in politics? If so, how?

10. Raise any points from the course booklet or CD/audiotape which haven't been covered in your discussion but which you feel strongly about.

In 2006 Archbishop Sentamu lived for a week in York Minster, praying and fasting for our hurting world.

6

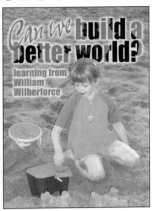

Can we build a better world?
learning from William Wilberforce

FRIENDSHIP & PRAYER:
then and now

> It might be said the moral transformation of the British Empire began in Holy Trinity Church. The Clapham Sect... combined evangelical fervour with hard-nosed political nous and excelled at mobilising a new generation of grassroots activists. Armed with Macaulay's first-hand accounts of the slave trade, they resolved to secure its abolition.
>
> *Professor Niall Ferguson*

Read about William Wilberforce and before long you bump into 'the Clapham Sect'. In today's world we don't like the word 'sect'. It conjures up images of brainwashing, indoctrination and spooky, manipulative leaders.

The Clapham Sect was far removed from all this. The term refers to a group of mainstream Anglican Christians who were evangelical in outlook and who met together to pray, to study the Bible, to plan, to encourage one another – and to enjoy each other's company.

Recently I ate lunch in an Oxford pub where, half a century ago, C S Lewis and JRR Tolkien met with other friends to share first drafts of *The Chronicles of Narnia, Lord of the Rings* and other stories. They called themselves 'The Inklings'. The Clapham Sect was a bit like that – though their concerns were religious and political, not literary. William Wilberforce was a leading member of that group.

Because the abolition of slavery in Britain is linked so strongly with William Wilberforce, it is easy to imagine that he achieved it on his own. He didn't!

John Newton, a former slave trader, had a profound influence on Wilberforce. Newton underwent a transforming conversion to Christ, which led to hymns such as *How sweet the name of Jesus sounds* and *Amazing Grace*. Thirty years older than Wilberforce, John Newton – himself an Anglican Minister – persuaded the young William to become an MP rather than a clergyman. Another clergyman – James Ramsey – also fostered Wilberforce's hatred of slavery.

And it was other influential Christian friends – men such as Henry Thornton (banker and politician), James Stephen (lawyer), Zachary Macaulay (one-time slave manager and Governor of Sierra Leone – and a founder of London University), Lord Teignmouth (ex-Governor-General of India) and John Venn – who worked tirelessly with Wilberforce on this great project. They attended Holy Trinity Church on Clapham Common, where John Venn was Rector from 1792 to 1813. Most members of the Clapham Sect were laymen.

Many of their close associates in the fight against slavery were Quakers. In 1787 the Society for the Abolition of the Slave Trade was founded, with Granville Sharp (an Anglican) as president of a mainly Quaker committee.

Encouragement In addition to those who worked alongside Wilberforce in his great struggle to build a better world – a world without slavery – a growing band of people encouraged from the sidelines. Most famous of these was John Wesley. Wesley had travelled widely in America as well as Britain, and he was a keen observer. His last known letter was written to Wilberforce. It contains this passionate exhortation: 'Go on in the name of God and in the power of his might, till even American slavery (the vilest that ever saw the sun) shall vanish away before it.'

John Wesley's encouragement must have meant a great deal to William Wilberforce.

*

One of the best-loved 'bit part' players in the New Testament is Barnabas, whose name means 'Son of Encouragement'. As I look back over my own life, I recognise the huge significance of that small army of people who have encouraged me – whether by a letter, a smile, a word in season, or even by a rebuke or vigorous debate.

As a young teacher, I began to sense God's call to the ordained ministry. I recall lengthy conversations with a senior church leader who gave me hours of his time. At that time I had little idea of just how busy he was. But he never seemed to be in a rush, as he listened carefully and spoke wisely. 'Encourage one another' urges St Paul (1 Thessalonians 5:11). Let's do more of it!

I have come to see friendship as one of God's greatest gifts. Happy the man who has a few close friends with whom he can share sorrows, joys, jokes, major concerns and the trivia of daily life. In my experience, women tend to be streets ahead of men in this respect – as in many others!

Of course, like all good gifts, friendship can be distorted. Peer pressure can lead us to adopt destructive attitudes and perform actions of which we are ashamed. This is particularly problematic for young people. I recall my anxious parents trying to extricate me (unsuccessfully!) from a group of 'dangerous' friends. While this can be a difficult and widespread problem for young people, negative pressures can exert themselves in adult life too.

Prayer

William Wilberforce and his friends in the Clapham Sect were men of prayer. They believed that through prayer they could listen to God and receive wisdom, guidance and the determination to press forward, despite setbacks and discouragements.

They also believed that through intercessory prayer, God would in some way act within the world – changing people's attitudes and making things happen. Did not Jesus himself assure us that faith can move mountains (Matthew 17:20)? They believed and acted upon that promise. They saw themselves as God's co-workers (1 Corinithians 3:9) as they worked tirelessly to build a better world.

We modern Christians tend to be happy with the first kind of prayer (the prayer of listening) but we are sometimes uneasy with the idea of praying in the expectation of concrete results. Might we perhaps learn from Wilberforce and his friends?

Work and Vision

For Wilberforce it was not a question of hard work *or* prayer, but hard work *and* prayer. Perhaps it is true that God helps those who help themselves. Any worthwhile endeavour – whether knitting a sweater or tending a garden – requires determination. Any great endeavour – whether writing a symphony or changing the world – requires vision. But the dream will only be fulfilled by hours, perhaps years, of hard work and attention to detail.

One of the greatest speeches of the twentieth century was based on a vision of a better world. *'I have a dream'*, declared Baptist pastor Martin Luther King. But turning the dream into reality involved numerous meetings, letters, speeches and marches. Eventually, his dream – which was built on William Wilberforce's vision of freedom – cost him his life.

In contrast, William Wilberforce enjoyed a long life. He retired in 1825 because of failing health and he lived for a further eight years. The 'Nightingale of The House of Commons' died on 29 July 1833, one month before his seventy-fourth birthday. He was buried in Westminster Abbey.

Wilberforce's conversion led him to rise above party, and to take into the political mainstream a whole series of causes: public hangings, the humanising of prison life, medical aid for the poor, and their education through the Charity and Sunday School movements. In 1796 the Bettering Society was formed to investigate problems engendered by poverty... The causes he espoused read like a roll call for the values of a new age.

Sir Roy Strong

QUESTIONS FOR GROUPS

BIBLE READING: Matthew 7:7-14

1. *Read 1 Samuel 20:41, 42.*
   (a) Do you agree that friendship is one of God's greatest gifts? Share experiences of enduring or influential friendships. **(b)** Do you agree that, in general, women are better at this than men? Tease out different approaches to friendship.

2. **(a)** William Wilberforce was a dazzling orator. But it is clear that he was a good listener too, for he heeded the advice of his friends and counsellors e.g. John Newton. Do you think that you are a good listener? What do your friends think? **(b)** What is the difference between listening and hearing? Do you know a really good listener – and what can you learn from him/her?

3. 'Encourage one another' (1 Thessalonians 5:11). As you look back over your life, can you describe a few people who have
   (a) encouraged you **(b)** inspired you **(c)** led you astray!
   How did they do this? What was the outcome (short and long term)?

4. Prayer involves making time to consciously put ourselves into the presence of God. Having done that, there are various kinds of prayer:
   - The prayer of penitence - *confession*
   - The prayer of adoration - *praise*
   - The prayer of gratitude - *thanksgiving*
   - The prayer of close attention - *listening*
   - The prayer of request - *intercession*
   - The prayer of fellowship - *corporate worship*
   - The prayer of despair - *lament*

   Share insights, difficulties, and encouragements arising from these different aspects of prayer.

5. *Read Philemon 1:22.* Can you give examples of answered prayer, from your own experience or from other people's?

6. In your experience, is it true that we modern believers are more comfortable with the prayer of listening than the prayer of asking? If so, do we need to rekindle the kind of faith which inspired Wilberforce and his friends – or were they naive?

7. Read the boxes by Thomas Merton, William Temple and Michael Ramsay (pages 8, 9). How do they relate to your view of life – and prayer?

8. *Read Joel 2:28-29 and Acts 2:17.* 'Stop daydreaming!' The Bible suggests that my schoolteacher was wrong. We *need* to dream if we are to build a better world (though not during maths lessons, I concede!). What, in your view, is the proper balance between inspiration and perspiration; between vision and detailed hard work?

9. *Read 1 Peter 2:9-12.*
   (a) When I was ordained some people said I was 'going into the Church'. In my view that's a terrible phrase! What do you think? **(b)** The influential Clapham Sect consisted mainly of laymen. Describe the balance between laity and clergy in your church. Has it shifted in recent years and have you got it about right?

10. Raise any points from the course booklet or CD/audiotape which haven't been covered in your discussion but which you feel strongly about.

God calls us [to build] his kingdom of love, peace and justice. On our own the task is daunting but together we can move mountains. Yes! On our own we can't get it together but together we can get it.
Archbishop Sentamu

SESSION 3

CHANGE & STRUGGLE: then and now

"Change and decay in all around I see
O Thou who changest not, abide with me"

So runs the famous, and rather lugubrious, hymn of Henry Francis Lyte.

True, not all change is for the better. Change can indeed give rise to decay. Many people in today's world (including some Christians) look back to 'the good old days.'

Wilberforce was an enemy of the status quo. He was an energetic agent for change in many key areas. The young MP saw that there was a great deal wrong with the society of his day and he was determined to make a difference. His driving ambition was to build a better world.

A man of his time

As we celebrate Wilberforce's immense achievements, others will 'knock' him. It's not difficult to smile at a man who helped form a 'Society for the reformation of manners.'* Of course he was a man of his time, and some of his attitudes seem very quaint to us – just as some of our attitudes will seem odd in a few years' time.

William Wilberforce set in train an immense agenda for change when he chose to combat the evils of slavery. The task must have seemed almost impossible, for the economy revolved around slavery and attitudes were deeply entrenched. But Wilberforce clung on to the word 'almost' and was prepared to devote much of his life to this great cause.

A modern parallel

Dame Cicely Saunders died in 2005. She, too, devoted her life to changing attitudes – not about slavery but about care for the dying. Her passion for change came about as a result of her experiences as a young nurse.

Like Wilberforce, she knew it would be a long, hard haul. I had the great privilege of interviewing Dame Cicely and she spoke about the importance of her Christian faith for the birth of the hospice movement. The obstacles to changing attitudes and approaches were so immense that she was tempted to give up. Cicely told me that it was the inspiration which she received from the teaching of Jesus Christ, and the strength she received from his Spirit within her, that kept her going.

I suspect that William Wilberforce would have said much the same.

> On 25 March 1807 the Abolition of the Slave Trade became law. But it was one thing to pass such an act and quite another to enforce it, added to which the optimistic belief that the planters would soon emancipate their slaves proved unfounded.
>
> *Sir Roy Strong*

---

* Note 'manners' means 'morals' in modern English

Resistance to change

From our vantage point in the twenty-first century, it's easy to be on the side of the angels. Of course, we would have supported Wilberforce! But would we? Most of us are resistant to change, especially when it causes inconvenience or leads to a fall in our standard of living.

His push for the abolition of slavery involved radical change. Inevitably this was resisted. Sadly, some church-goers opposed him. Lord Nelson was among his many influential opponents. The path was not easy.

Change in today's world

If we are to honour and celebrate William Wilberforce properly, we will follow his example. What are the issues in today's world which need to be tackled and changed? We turn to some of these now.

First and foremost are the issues outlined in Session 1. These include modern slavery; exploiting those on the edges of society; unfair trading practices; Making Poverty History; providing clean water for all; ensuring that schools and hospitals in earthquake areas are built safely; tackling widespread diseases like malaria, TB, HIV/Aids and leprosy with greater vigour and increased resources. And, of course, there is the ever-present threat of terrorism.

Most people would agree with this short list but, as with slavery 200 years ago, opinion is divided about many other issues, including the following:

- **The media** TV has come a long way since the days of *Andy Pandy* and *Bill and Ben the Flowerpot Men*. So have films. The producer of *Gone with the Wind* (1939) had to get permission to end his epic with the famous remark, 'Frankly, my dear, I don't give a damn'.

In early movies actors could appear in bed together only if they kept one foot on the floor!

Ava Gardner's first starring role was in *The Killers* (1946). Scenes showing drinking, an unmade bed and a man stripped to the waist were all cut by the censor.

Today, four letter words abound, as do bosoms and backsides. All this is in stark contrast to William Wilberforce and his campaign for the reformation of manners. Is this liberating? Or has it all gone too far, too fast?

- **Marriage and family life** In Wilberforce's day, divorce was virtually impossible for most people. In contrast, one in three marriages in Britain ends that

CAN WE BUILD A BETTER WORLD?
learning from William Wilberforce

with **Archbishop John Sentamu**
Wendy Craig
Leslie Griffiths
Closing Reflections by
Five Poor Clares from BBC TV's The Convent
Introduced by
Dr David Hope

FIVE SESSIONS: *Slavery: then and now; Friendship & Prayer: then and now; Change & Struggle: then and now; The Bible: then and now; Redemption & Restitution: then and now*

WHERE IS GOD...?

with **Archbishop Rowan Williams**
Patricia Routledge CBE
Joel Edwards
Dr Pauline Webb

Introduced by
Dr David Hope

FIVE SESSIONS: **Where is God...? when we** ... *try to make sense of life? ... seek happiness? ... face suffering? ... make decisions? ... contemplate death?*

> **"This is the best course this year for Lent groups to use."**
>
> Church Times review (2006)

BETTER TOGETHER?

with
Abbot of Ampleforth
John Bell
Nicky Gumbel
Jane Williams

Introduced by
Dr David Hope

FIVE SESSIONS: *Family Relationships; Church Relationships; Relating to Strangers; Broken Relationships; Our Relationship with God*

TOUGH TALK
Hard Sayings of Jesus

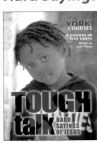

with
Bishop Tom Wright
Steve Chalke
Fr Gerard Hughes SJ
Prof Frances Young

Introduced by
Dr David Hope

FIVE SESSIONS: *Shrinking and Growing; Giving and Using; Praying and Forgiving; Loving and Telling; Trusting and Entering*

> **"I think that these courses are some of the best things that the Church of England has produced over the years "**
>
> Dr David Hope

PRICES FOR THE ABOVE COURSES

BOOKLET: £3.50 *(£2.75 each for 5 or more)*
TAPE: £8.95 *(£6.95 each for 5 or more)*
CD: £10.95 *(£8.95 each for 3 or more)*
TRANSCRIPT: £5.00

ALL OF OUR PRICES INCLUDE PACKING AND SECOND CLASS POSTAGE

NEW WORLD, OLD FAITH

with
**Archbishop
   Rowan Williams
David Coffey
Joel Edwards
Revd Dr John
   Polkinghorne** KBE FRS
Dr Pauline Webb

Introduced by **Dr David Hope**

FIVE SESSIONS: *Brave New World?;
Environment and Ethics; Church and
Family in Crisis?; One World – Many
Faiths; Spirituality and Superstition*

IN THE WILDERNESS

with
**Cardinal Cormac
   Murphy-O'Connor
Archbishop
   David Hope
Revd Dr Rob Frost
Roy Jenkins
Dr Elaine Storkey**

FIVE SESSIONS: *Jesus, Satan and
the Angels; The Wilderness Today;
The Church in the Wilderness; Prayer,
Meditation and Scripture; Solitude,
Friendship and Fellowship*

FAITH IN THE FIRE

with
**Archbishop
   David Hope
Rabbi Lionel Blue
Steve Chalke
Revd Dr Leslie
   Griffiths
Ann Widdecombe** MP

FIVE SESSIONS: *Faith facing Facts;
Faith facing Doubt; Faith facing Disaster;
Faith fuelling Prayer; Faith fuelling Action*

JESUS REDISCOVERED

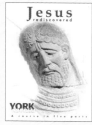

with
Paul Boateng MP
**Dr Lavinia Byrne
Joel Edwards
Bishop Tom Wright
Archbishop
   David Hope**

FIVE SESSIONS: *Jesus' Life and
Teaching; Following Jesus; Jesus: Saviour
of the World; Jesus is Lord; Jesus and the
Church*

*Ideally, each group member should have their
own booklet. To help make this possible, we reduce
the price per booklet when you buy 5 or more.*

PRICES FOR THE ABOVE COURSES

BOOKLET:	£3.50	(**£2.75** each for 5 or more)
TAPE:	£8.95	(**£6.95** each for 5 or more)
TRANSCRIPT:	£5.00	

*ALL OF OUR
PRICES INCLUDE
PACKING AND
SECOND CLASS
POSTAGE*

" *The format works brilliantly.* **"** Church Times review

ATTENDING, EXPLORING, ENGAGING with

**Archbishop David Hope;
Steve Chalke; Fr Gerard Hughes SJ;
Professor Frances Young**

TAPE: £8.95
(£6.95 each for 5 or more)

PHOTOCOPYABLE NOTES: £2.50

FIVE SESSIONS: *Attending to God;
Attending to One Another; Exploring Our
Faith; Engaging with the World in Service;
Engaging with the World in Evangelism*

THE TEACHING OF JESUS with

**Steve Chalke; Professor James Dunn;
Dr Pauline Webb; Archbishop David Hope**

TAPE: £8.95
(£6.95 each for 5 or more)

PHOTOCOPYABLE NOTES: £2.50

FIVE SESSIONS: *Forgiveness; God;
Money; Heaven and Hell; On Being Human*

GREAT EVENTS, DEEP MEANINGS with

Revd Dr John Polkinghorne KBE FRS;
**Gordon Wilson;
David Konstant** - RC Bishop of Leeds;
**Fiona Castle; Dame Cicely Saunders;
Archbishop David Hope**

TAPE: £8.95
(£6.95 each for 5 or more)

PHOTOCOPYABLE NOTES: £2.50

SIX SESSIONS: *Christmas; Ash Wednesday;
Palm Sunday; Good Friday; Easter; Pentecost*

LIVE YOUR FAITH with

**Revd Dr Donald English; Lord Tonypandy;
Fiona & Roy Castle**

TAPE: £8.95
(£6.95 each for 5 or more)

BOOKLET (black & white): £3.50
(£2.75 each for 5 or more)

SIX SESSIONS: *Jesus; Prayer; the Church;
the Holy Spirit; the Bible; Service and Witness*

Also – TOPIC TAPES for individual listening

STRUGGLING/ COPING

TAPE 1: £5.00
*Living with **depression**
Living with **panic attacks***

TAPE 2: £5.00
*Living with **cancer**
Living with **bereavement**
Four personal conversations*

SCIENCE AND CHRISTIAN FAITH

£5.00

An in-depth discussion with
the **Revd Dr John
Polkinghorne** KBE FRS,
former Professor of
Mathematical Physics at
Cambridge University

EVANGELISM TODAY £5.00

with contributions by
Canon Robin Gamble, the
**Revd Brian Hoare, Bishop
Gavin Reid** and **Canon
Robert Warren**

FINDING FAITH £1.20
(95p each for 10 or more)

is a twenty-minute
audiotape, designed for
enquirers and church
members. Four brief stories
by people, including
Archbishop David Hope,
who have found faith.

*Inexpensive! Designed as a
'give away'*

PRAYER £3.50
(£2.50 each for 5 or more)

SIDE 1:
Archbishop David Hope
on *Prayer*

SIDE 2:
Four Christians on praying
*... for healing; in danger; in
tongues; with perseverance*

This tape accompanies the
booklet *The Archbishop's
School of Prayer (see details
overleaf)*

NO HIDDEN EXTRAS!
*All our prices include
packing and second
class postage*

Archbishop's School Series

7 BOOKLETS COMMISSIONED BY ARCHBISHOP DAVID HOPE

- Prayer
- Bible Reading
- Evangelism
- The Sacraments
- Christianity and Science
- Healing and Wholeness
- Life After Death

- Single copy – **£1.25p**
- 2-19 copies – **£1.10p** each
- 20+ copies – **95p** each
- 50+ copies – **75p** each
- 100+ copies – **62p** each

The Archbishop's School of the Sacraments

Written by Simon Stanley

Living the Gospel

* Authors include John Polkinghorne and David Winter

SPECIAL OFFER

You may order a complete set of all seven booklets for only £5.

The Archbishop's School of Prayer

TRANSCRIPTS

A word-by-word transcript is available for *Can we build a better world?* as a separate booklet in an easy-to-follow format.

TRANSCRIPTS enable group members to:
- *follow the conversation on the CD/audiotape*
- *read the dialogue before or after each session*

TRANSCRIPTS are particularly helpful for:
- *GROUP LEADERS when preparing*
- *anyone with hearing difficulties*

TRANSCRIPTS are available for several of our courses at £5.00 per copy – please look for the symbol and state TRANSCRIPT when ordering

Books by John Young *(co-founder of York Courses)*
John has work in several languages including Chinese and Russian

JOURNEYS INTO FAITH

A4 workbook for groups to encourage effective outreach

Published by *Churches Together in England* and *The Bible Society*

Was **£7.99** now **£2.50**

SPECIAL £7.99 **£2.50** OFFER

THE CASE AGAINST CHRIST
Fully revised in 2006

John Young acts as Counsel for the Defence in the Case against Christ.

"A classic" *Nicky Gumbel*
"John Young has a great gift for communicating profound ideas simply and readably"
Archbishop John Habgood

£7.99

TEACH YOURSELF CHRISTIANITY

An introduction to Christianity as a living faith.
"not only informs, it excites" *Dr David Hope*
"… this important book" *Bishop James Jones*
"An amazing compilation. Brilliant!"
Dr Peter Brierley

£8.99 Published by *Hodder & Stoughton*

PLEASE NOTE OUR NEW CONTACT NUMBERS!

YORK COURSES

York Courses · PO Box 343 · York YO19 5YB
Tel: 01904 466516 · Fax: 01904 630577
email: courses@yorkcourses.co.uk
website: www.yorkcourses.co.uk

Payment with order please. Cheques: York Courses
All prices include packing & second class postage in the UK

way today. Co-habitation is common and being 'born out of wedlock' no longer carries a stigma. All this has accelerated over the past three decades. Have these changes added to the sum of human happiness – or to human misery?

- **Respect** In 2005 George Galloway launched a new political party called *Respect*, and Tony Blair's government announced that it was focusing on 'respect'. At the same time cartoonists, playwrights and others lampooned cherished beliefs.

Free speech and robust argument are vitally important. But does this involve throwing sensitivity in the dustbin? And what if insensitivity leads to violence? What action might be appropriate? That is a challenging question. Would you side with Sikhs demonstrating against a play which shows them in a bad light? Or with Muslim women who demand the right to be fully-veiled? Did you march with Muslims protesting against cartoons which depicted the Prophet Muhammad as a terrorist? And how do you feel about Christians who picket theatres playing *Jerry Springer, the Opera,* or cinemas showing *The Da Vinci Code,* on the grounds that they insult Jesus?

- **Political Correctness** This is related to respect. 'PC' gets a bad press, and it does sometimes seem like madness. But I want to swim against the stream by asserting that, at root, political correctness is a *good* thing. At its best it is a bid for respect and sensitivity. Yes, we may have taken it too far, but I think I understand why some women don't want to be called 'sons' of God, why some black people call themselves Afro-Caribbean and why we should not be allowed to deny the Holocaust. Words and attitudes matter, as well as actions.

- **Church worship** In many churches, worship has changed out of all recognition over the last forty years. Most Christians now address God as 'You' not 'Thou'; laughing and clapping in church are common (the latter encouraged by Pope John Paul II); dress is often informal. All very different from my Sunday-school days!

Another noticeable difference is numerical: there are fewer of us. And we are more likely to rub shoulders with people of other faiths. The Christian faith no longer has a privileged position in British society. Indeed, writers and comedians are more likely to poke fun at Christianity than at other faiths, finding it to be a softer target.

- **Climate change** Many informed commentators believe this to be the biggest question of all. It simply wasn't an issue for William Wilberforce, who lived much of his life before the industrial revolution. But it is an immense dilemma for us – and will be an even bigger problem for our grandchildren.

Like it or not it seems that we shall all have to change our ways – the climate itself will see to that. The question is: are we willing to make the necessary *voluntary* changes needed to save our planet – especially as these may be very radical.

Some politicians, mainly American, refuse to accept the strength of the evidence for climate change. In contrast, some informed observers believe that, whatever we do, we may already be too late to preserve our present way of life. The influential Professor James Lovelock (of 'Gaia' fame) believes that we must shift our focus from *preventing* climate change, to *managing* its far-reaching consequences. The Government's Chief Scientist, Professor Sir David King, seemed to endorse this, when in April 06 he predicted a global rise in temperature of around 3°C by the end of this century.

To make this vast issue more personal perhaps we should ponder this question. Will our children's children despise us for leaving them a dangerous and inhospitable world?

QUESTIONS FOR GROUPS
BIBLE READING: Malachi 3:6-7 and Matthew 18:3

1. Look back to your childhood. What are the most striking changes in the world at large that have taken place since then? Which of these do you welcome? Which of these do you regret?

2. How about the Church? Some churches have changed very little over the past 50 years, while others are very different indeed. **(a)** Has your church changed much since you joined? **(b)** Which changes did you or do you resist? **(c)** Which additional changes would you still like to make?

3. **(a)** Wilberforce lived in a world without radio, TV or internet – and with fewer books too. How would you cope without these? **(b)** They are a huge blessing but raise immense problems too as producers, editors, authors and bloggers push the boundaries of what's acceptable. There *are* limits on free speech in modern Britain e.g. stirring up racial hatred is illegal. Where would you draw the lines? In your view, have the boundaries (sex, hatred, violence, swearing on TV...) been crossed? **(c)** Is public protest sensible (e.g. Jerry Springer; *The Da Vinci Code* film) or does it provide 'the oxygen of publicity'? **(d)** Do you agree that Christianity is a softer target (e.g. for comedians, film makers) than other faiths? And if so, why?

4. *Read Exodus 20:8-11.*
   (a) Do you welcome or regret the increasing pace of life? How do you

build silence and stillness into your daily life, if you do? **(b)** How do you feel about the changing face of Sunday? Despite the commercialisation of Sunday, how can/should Christians make space for God, prayer, reflection and family?

5. *Read Ephesians 5:21 and 6:1-9.*
   (a) The 'deferential society' is dead. Does this make you sad or glad? **(b)** Has respect disappeared with deference? If so, can respect be restored, and how? **(c)** Does the fear of terrorism impact upon your life? If so, in what ways?

6. Do you agree/disagree with the comments about political correctness on page 13. Can you give examples of PC which seem to you to be **(a)** silly **(b)** sensible.

7. Climate change is a huge issue and building a better world means leaving a *safer* world.
   (a) Imagine and describe a world in which sea levels have risen by 1 to 3 metres. **(b)** What changes in lifestyle are you making – or do you feel helpless to do anything useful? **(c)** What changes do you think governments should impose upon us?

8. **(a)** List the changes to family life in your lifetime. Are these changes for better or for worse, in your view? **(b)** Should divorce be made more difficult? Does easier divorce make for greater happiness or greater misery, in your opinion – for adults and/or for children?

9. *Read Matthew 28:20.* The risen Lord promises to be with us throughout the decades and centuries. What difference does this belief make to you in a fast moving world? Which other aspects of your faith bring peace and calm in the midst of rapid change?

10. Raise any points from the course booklet or CD/audiotape which haven't been covered in your discussion but which you feel strongly about.

We place no emphasis now on the spiritual. We sneer at the spiritual. We sneer at Christianity. We sneer at any concept of self-restraint.   *Ann Widdecombe*

Poor Clares devote their lives to praying for our hurting world.

SESSION 4

THE BIBLE:
then and now

Interviewees on BBC Radio 4's *Desert Island Discs* are told that they will have a Bible and the complete works of Shakespeare on their imaginary desert island. One participant responded that the Bible would be useful for lighting fires. Clearly he felt that this old book has little to say to the modern world – apart, perhaps, from encouraging racial and territorial wars.

In contrast, Wilberforce and his friends in the Clapham Sect were men of the Bible. They read it, studied it and committed it to memory. They rejoiced in its message and attempted to live by its precepts. It was the inspiration behind their campaign against slavery. It was their blueprint for building a better world.

Since their time, the Bible has been subjected to intense scrutiny by generations of fine minds and we are aware of a raft of fascinating – and sometimes difficult – questions which were not around in Wilberforce's day. We also understand its background and formation far better. And we are even more aware of its power to convert and sustain – an additional aspect of their legacy to us.

Wilberforce was passionate about the abolition of slavery but he was not a single-issue Christian. He involved himself energetically in a raft of concerns, including the foundation of the Church Missionary Society in 1799 (now called the Church Mission Society – CMS) and the Bible Society in 1804. He believed that the Bible was 'more powerful than a two-edged sword' (Hebrews 4:12). For William Wilberforce it was nothing less than the Word of God.

So he set about making it widely available through the formation of the British and Foreign Bible Society – now spread around the globe as the United Bible Societies. Stories about the transforming power of the Scriptures have flooded back to Britain from every continent.

From all this, three key points emerge:

1. An encouraging book

In a previous York course entitled *Where is God....?* we invited the Archbishop of Canterbury, Joel Edwards and the actress Patricia Routledge to explore life's 'big questions'. Where is God when we seek happiness, face suffering, make decisions, and contemplate death? The final question they considered was: 'Where is God when we try to make sense of life?'.

The Bible explores this deep and important question at length and with great profundity. Job grapples with the tension raised by his belief in a powerful God and his personal experience of a suffering world. Ecclesiastes explores what it feels like to live in a world without meaning.

But grasp the Bible's central themes and your spirit soars. The Scriptures affirm that we are not here on earth simply by blind chance. We do not bumble around for 70 years or so, only to fall off the edge into oblivion. No, we have been *loved* into existence – and it is God's love which will carry us beyond the doors of death and through the gates of glory.

At the centre of the Bible's message is the key notion of *grace*. The 'glad tidings of great joy' are not only for good people but for *all* people – including you and me. Above all, the Bible brings good news to moral and spiritual failures. Its strategy for failure is focused in the death and resurrection of Jesus Christ. Jesus himself declared his death to be 'a ransom for many' (Mark 10:45). By this drastic means he sets us free – free from fear, from sin, and from death.

This extraordinary contradiction – a dying man saving the world – is, according to the New Testament, the open secret at the heart of the universe. It is 'the foolishness of God' which is 'wiser than man's wisdom' (1 Corinthians 1:25). This breathtaking assertion is vindicated at Easter when the Church worldwide rejoices in the resurrection of Jesus and declares:

Alleluia! Christ is risen
He is risen indeed. Alleluia!

2. A sustaining book

The Bible is not a work of theory, unrelated to the messiness, mystery and majesty of life. It tells a great story and contains some difficult passages. At the same time the Bible is very practical. It is a proven resource, designed to provide wisdom for living in an imperfect world. It contains the secret of happiness – and much more besides.

As with the cross, this secret is contained within a deep contradiction. Live generously. Give yourself away. Do this joyfully in the service of others. Only then will you find your true self.

The Bible has enduring power to sustain us in the bleakest circumstances. From numerous possible examples, I will choose just one.*

---

* Taken from the recently revised edition of *The Case Against Christ* (Hodder Paperback by John Young with David Wilkinson)

17

> If all the neglected Bibles were dusted at the same time we would have a record dust storm and the sun would go into eclipse for a whole week.
>
> *David Nygren*

> Whoever made this Book, made me. It knows all that is in my heart.
>
> *A Chinese reader of the Bible*

> When the missionaries came to Africa the Africans had the land and the missionaries had the Bible. They told us to close our eyes and pray and when we opened our eyes, they had the land and we had the Bible. We had the better deal.
>
> *Archbishop Desmond Tutu*

Martin Niemoeller was a German pastor in the Confessing Church during World War II. Like his colleague Dietrich Bonhoeffer, he was imprisoned. Unlike Bonhoeffer, he survived Hitler's madness. Indeed, I had the great privilege of hearing him speak some thirty years after the end of the war. When he got enthusiastic he broke into German. The meeting's chairman, the Earl of March, had to intervene: 'Martin, you're speaking German', he said gently. The speaker then resumed in fluent English!

This is what he wrote about his imprisonment. It reveals, in a warm and inspiring way, the sustaining power of the Scriptures:

> *'What did the Bible mean to me during the long weary years of solitary confinement, and then for the last 4 years [in Dachau concentration camp]. The Word of God was simply everything to me - comfort and strength, guidance and hope, master of my days and companion of my nights, the bread which kept me from starvation, and the water of life which refreshed my soul'.*

3. A challenging book

The Bible is not a book of personal piety. Its stress on God's grace is balanced by its call for human transformation. Yes, it brings great comfort. But it brings disturbing challenge too, and its message is for national life as well as individual lives.

The prophets insisted on social justice. The Bible is political in the sense that it commands the nations' leaders to take special care of the poor, the vulnerable and the marginalised. Foreigners, orphans and widows are frequently mentioned in its pages, for they were most at risk in the ancient world. So Archbishop Desmond Tutu can declare: 'I am puzzled about which Bible people are reading when they suggest religion and politics don't mix'. He goes on to assert that God is very interested indeed in the way we organise society. But, of course, political does not mean 'party political'.

In recent years, Liberation Theology has become a powerful – and controversial – force, especially in Latin America. Some Liberation theologians have been accused of being more Marxist than Christian. They have a special concern for those who are living in slums and on rubbish dumps. They draw on the book of Exodus which describes the Israelites' escape from servitude in Egypt – a theme very close to the heart of William Wilberforce.

QUESTIONS FOR GROUPS

BIBLE READING: Psalm 19:7-14

1. Read a favourite Bible passage to other members of your group and explain why you chose it.

2. Invite a few members of your group to sum up the central message of the Bible in a sentence or two. Discuss these suggestions, and the participants' suggestions on the CD/audiotape.

3. *Read John 1:14, 17 and 2 Corinthians 5:17.* Two key Bible themes are *grace* and *transformation*. Read John Newton's famous hymn *Amazing Grace* out loud. What do you understand by 'grace'? Do you share Newton's understanding i.e. do you feel yourself to be a 'wretch' and 'lost' without the grace of God?

4. Re-read Martin Niemoeller's comments (page 18). What do you make of them? Have you felt the comfort and inspiration of the Bible's guidance or influence at critical moments in your own life? Share experiences.

5. **(a)** Does the Bible have a place in your own life, outside a church service? (Note: recent research shows that the Bible is a neglected best-seller, even among churchgoers, so don't be embarrassed if you fall into this category!). **(b)** Would you like to read a short passage every day or every week? If so, see below.

6. If Desmond Tutu and many others are right (see page 18), the Bible is highly political. What do you understand by this?

7. Discuss the boxes in this session. Pick out two which 'speak' to you.

8. *Read Psalm 23:1, Psalm 121 and Romans 8:28 (see also, verses 31 and 32).*
What might these passages mean for you *today* – as an individual, group or church?

9. *Read Exodus 22:21 and Psalm 146:9.* What bearing, if any, should this teaching have on Britain's immigration policy and our attitude to refugees?

10. Raise any points from the course booklet or CD/audiotape which haven't been covered in your discussion but which you feel strongly about.

● Try reading suitable parts of the Bible as lovingly as possible – lingering over the scene, noticing every detail as if you had been there, asking what it shows you of God. Such 'meditation' on the Bible supplies a solid basis for prayer – and life. When you have got clearer in your mind the reality of God, coming to you in Jesus, stepping out of the pages of the Bible, you will find it easier to put together the jigsaw puzzle of your life.

David L Edwards

● There are many schemes designed to help with daily Bible reading. *The Bible Reading Fellowship, Scripture Union* and *Every Day with Jesus* take a few verses and offer comments. *Living Light* does the same and provides an attractive booklet free of charge (01277 365398). *York Courses* have published a booklet *The Archbishop's School of Bible Reading* (written by John Young, author of this course), designed to encourage the hesitant.

SESSION 5

Can we **build a better world?**

learning from William Wilberforce

REDEMPTION & RESTITUTION: then and now

Granville Sharp, the Bible Society's first chairman, found Jonathon Strong, abandoned by his master and suffering from vicious beatings. He secured medical treatment and work for him, before Strong's former owner legally challenged Sharp for the return of his 'property'. Sharp then went to court (1772) and won Strong his freedom – a landmark victory.

In this final session we pick up some of the related themes which have emerged since that Westminster Act of Parliament abolished the Slave Trade on 25 March 1807.

Attitudes to Slavery

It is significant – and not a little puzzling – that Wilberforce drew his inspiration from the Bible, for the Christian Scriptures accept slavery as a fact of life. In the New Testament St Paul writes a very tender, short letter to a slave owner called Philemon. He writes on behalf of Onesimus, a runaway slave, asking Philemon to receive him back as a beloved brother. Paul does not rebuke Philemon for owning slaves. Instead, he sows the seeds for the abolition of slavery itself.

The apostle insists that in the Church believers are 'all one in Christ Jesus' (Galatians 3:28) regardless of race, gender, colour or social status. In the ancient world this seemed both revolutionary and ridiculous. At Holy Communion, all were equal as they ate bread and drank wine together – and this included slaves and their masters. Such 'absurd' equality was found nowhere else in the Graeco-Roman world. And, of course, the theory didn't always work perfectly in practice.

But it was this teaching which convinced William Wilberforce that the God of the Bible was urging him on in his great campaign. For the New Testament sowed seeds which caused a fundamental shift in attitudes towards slavery. Christian slave owners in New Testament times came to view their slaves as brothers and sisters, not simply as possessions. This new mindset could not be resisted, and would have far-reaching consequences.

Other seeds for radical change

This 'seed sowing' function of the Bible applies to other areas of life too – attitudes towards children and women, for example.

The Scriptures were written over many centuries, by men, in societies which were marked by male domination. It cannot be denied that the Scriptures reflect this. At the same time, the radical respect and tenderness shown by Jesus towards women sowed important seeds of change. Despite the bad press received by St Paul in this regard, close reading of the New Testament also shows his immense regard for women – and his dependence on them, both personally and in spreading the gospel. Dr Pauline Webb certainly thinks so:

'I find it quite astonishing that St Paul should be regarded as a male chauvinist. Like Jesus himself, Paul had a great respect for women and regarded them as among his closest colleagues... Far from being reactionary, Paul was, like Jesus, revolutionary in his personal dealings with women.'

Moving to another area, Professor Basil Mitchell has pointed out that the Bible was an important influence in the founding of modern democracies. He argues that the very notion of a liberal democratic state 'owes its existence very largely to Christianity in its Protestant forms and rests upon certain values of freedom and the worth of persons which are authentically, if not exclusively, Christian'. The Reformation stress on 'the priesthood of all believers', based on New Testament teaching, certainly sowed seeds which we recognise today in the modern stress on individualism – for good or for ill!

Redemption

The Big Issue is a huge publishing success. The cover picture of Issue 684 featured a beautiful young woman with the heading 'Mary J. Blige: the drink, the drugs, the abuse, the redemption'.

The article speaks of a transformation in the life of the singer: 'It may be five years since she cleaned up her act, but struggle and redemption still resonate on... Song titles like *Gonna Break Through; Take me as I am*; and *Baggage* speak for themselves.'

As this illustrates, *redemption* is one of the great Bible words which continues to play an important role in modern thought.

Redemption carries overtones of salvation, transformation and new life. As we saw in Session 4, the Bible makes clear that Jesus is the Redeemer who gave his life 'as a ransom for many' (Mark 10:45). This can only be understood against the background of slavery in New Testament times. It was possible for slaves to be 'redeemed' – set free – on payment of a ransom price. When this happened a new life opened up in which former slaves could make decisions, earn money and live independent lives.

The New Testament insists that we are all enslaved to habits and attitudes from which we need to be liberated. Talk of 'salvation from sin' can sound very religious and conveniently far-removed from our everyday lives. The Scripture makes clear that its teaching is intensely *practical*. We need to be 'saved from sin' not only in a general sense but in hard-hitting detail. God wants to work with us on our greed, our tetchiness, our lust, our timidity, our jealousy, our love of gossiping, our...

He wants us to tackle, with his help, all those things
which diminish us and make life difficult for those with
whom we live, work and play. David L Edwards, former
Dean of Norwich Cathedral, makes this point very
pithily: "By dying like that, Jesus has won the right to be
'Our Lord'. The word 'Lord' here means 'Boss' ... There
are many ways of defining what 'a Christian' is. The best
one is this: a Christian is one who takes orders from
Jesus Christ as Lord."

If redemption is to take place, then we need the power
of the Risen Christ within us. Jesus Christ offers us this
new life – abundant life – but he insists that we embrace
new values. These are the values of the Kingdom of God,
summed up by Jesus in the Fourth Gospel where he told
his disciples to 'Love one another as I have loved you'.

No doubt, in the days of the Roman Empire, some
ransomed slaves thought twice before accepting their
freedom. In their present life they had had no freedom
but they were provided with food, clothes and shelter.
And they were spared from taking tough decisions. In
the new life on offer, these advantages would not be part
of the package. Freedom is risky stuff! So Jesus insists
that we count the cost before embarking on a life of
discipleship.

Restoration and restitution

In 2006, the General Synod of the Church of England
debated slavery. A motion before Synod urged the
Church to apologise for the part it played in the slave
trade. We can gather from this proposal that not all
Wilberforce's fellow Christians were as passionate in
their loathing of slavery as he was.

After vigorous debate, the Synod motion was passed. But
all this raises significant issues. Is it possible for us to
apologise, in any meaningful sense, for the sins of those
who lived over two hundred years ago? Can we do
anything to bring about reconciliation and restitution,
as far as the descendents of slaves are concerned? Is it
right – and is it reasonable – to ask the modern-day
descendents of eighteenth-century slaves to forgive us
for 'the sins of our fathers'?

For one thing, slavery wasn't a simple matter of black
versus white. We certainly cannot escape the fact that
'white nations' were the main culprits. But some African
leaders readily co-operated, for slavery made them
wealthy too.

> He who would do good to another, must do it in Minute Particulars.
>
> *William Blake*

Restitution is a hot issue in today's world. Those black-and-white Cowboy versus Indian films which I loved as a child, and played out with my friends in the school playground, raise immense and wide-ranging problems. How should modern white Americans relate to those from whom, at least on one reading of history, they 'stole' land? And what about the Maoris in New Zealand and the Aborigines in Australia?

For that matter, what about Britain's possession of the Elgin Marbles? Doesn't Greece have a strong case in demanding their return? Indeed, should the British Museum return all its other treasures to their many countries of origin?

William Wilberforce Esqr M.P.

Criminals and their victims

In our justice system 'restorative justice' is increasingly practised. Its advocates argue that it can be very effective to arrange a meeting between criminals and their victims. At face value it does seem more productive to confront perpetrators with the damaging effects of their actions than simply to lock them away.

These issues – and many more – demand attention as we reflect on the world we have inherited from William Wilberforce and his colleagues. Deep questions are raised for us as disciples of Jesus Christ. As we give thanks for their inspiration, let us tremble, too, at the challenge they present to us, as we seek to build a better world.

One thing, at least, is very clear – without the influence of Wilberforce and his Christian friends *then*, our world would be very different *now*.

All good wishes as you grapple with these important issues.

QUESTIONS FOR GROUPS

BIBLE READING: 1 Peter 1:17-25

1. Wilberforce's friend (see BOX on page 21) clearly appreciated his laughter. Draw up a list of characteristics you like in *your* friends. How important is humour and laughter? How important is a shared faith?

2. In recent years Britain has celebrated several important anniversaries – the Battle of Trafalgar, the end of the Second World War, the Queen's 80th birthday, and the abolition of the slave trade. What significance do such anniversaries have for our nation and – more personally – what do family anniversaries mean to group members?

3. *Read Hebrews 12:1.* Catholics have their saints and Protestants their heroes. The New Testament encourages us to look at those great men and women of faith and draw strength for our own discipleship. What encouragement do you draw from William Wilberforce, from other great Christians, and from your Christian friends?

4. *Read Matthew 1:21.* Re-read together the section headed 'Redemption' (page 21). Do you agree that the Christian doctrine of redemption is severely practical and challenging to every Christian? Share insights from personal experience.

5. England, Scotland, Wales and Ireland each has its own patron saint, but Britain itself does not. Imagine that the United Kingdom is looking for a patron saint – who needn't be an official 'saint'. Draw up a short list of candidates. Would you include Wilberforce? Can your group agree on just *one* name?

6. Where does your group go from here? Disband maybe? Meet for another course in the future? Meet regularly perhaps? Or could you look outwards and see if you might invite others to join you – perhaps for discussion, perhaps for a meal or an outing...?

7. Is it sensible and possible to apply the principle of restitution to national issues like slavery, land rights, the Elgin Marbles and other historical treasures? Or should we let bygones be bygones and simply 'move on'?

8. What about restorative justice? Imagine you've been burgled – losing money and items with sentimental value. The thief is imprisoned. Would you wish to meet him/her in order to confront them with the hurt they have inflicted? Or would you find that too disturbing?

9. This is your final chance to raise any other points from the booklet, CD/audiotape or to revisit areas covered in previous weeks.

10. Well, *can* we build a better world?

The whole substance of religion is faith, hope and love... all things are possible to him who believes, they are less difficult to him who hopes, they are more easy to him who loves, and still more easy to him who perseveres in the practice of these three virtues.

Brother Lawrence – Carmelite lay brother (c.1605-91)

PARTICIPANTS
on the CD/audiotape:

- **DR JOHN SENTAMU,** a former High Court Judge in Uganda, is the 97th Archbishop of York.
- **WENDY CRAIG** is a widely known and well-loved actress, whose television roles include the scatty mother in *Butterflies* and Matron in *The Royal*. Wendy has been a committed Christian for several years.
- **THE REVD DR LESLIE GRIFFITHS** – now Lord Griffiths – is a leading Methodist and Minister of Wesley's Chapel in London. His is a familiar voice on BBC Radio 4's *Thought for the Day* and *The Daily Service*.
- **POOR CLARE SISTERS** from Arundel, who featured in BBC TV's popular documentary series *The Convent*, give the Closing Reflections on the CD/audiotape.
- **DR DAVID HOPE** introduces the course. He was Archbishop of York from 1995 to 2005.

THE AUTHOR

This course booklet is written by the Revd Canon John Young, author of twenty books and co-founder of *York Courses*. His work has been translated into several languages, including Chinese and Russian.

YORK COURSES

- founded in Lent 1997
- widely used in Britain and throughout the world
- committed to ecumenical activity and to honest exploration, sharing and deepening of faith
- produced by Simon Stanley (Archbishop of York's adviser for York City Centre Churches, parish priest and former BBC producer/presenter) and John Young (see author details above). Both are Canons of York Minster.

John Young

Simon Stanley

Elaine Stanley, Administrator

A FIVE PART COURSE
for groups and individuals

Featuring on CD/audiotape
- **Archbishop John Sentamu**
- **Wendy Craig**
- **Leslie Griffiths**
- **Five Poor Clares from BBC TV's *The Convent* (Reflections)**
- **Introduced by Dr David Hope, former Archbishop of York**

See inside this cover for details of the participants

Can we build a better world?

1. **SLAVERY:** then and now
2. **FRIENDSHIP & PRAYER:** then and now
3. **CHANGE & STRUGGLE:** then and now
4. **THE BIBLE:** then and now
5. **REDEMPTION & RESTITUTION:** then and now

This **BOOKLET** accompanies the **CD/AUDIOTAPE** also entitled *Can we build a better world?*

A word-by-word **TRANSCRIPT** of the CD/audiotape is also available.

> *... these courses are some of the best things that the Church of England has produced ...*
>
> Dr David Hope, Archbishop of York 1995-2005

ISBN 0-9546728-5-2

ISBN 978-0-9546728-5-0

9 780954 672850

YORK COURSES

York Courses · PO Box 343 · York YO19 5YB Tel : 01904 466516
Fax: 01904 630577
email: courses@yorkcourses.co.uk
www.yorkcourses.co.uk